AF487403

THIS JOURNAL BELONGS TO

____

MONDAY
DEAR DIARY

TUESDAY
DEAR DIARY

WEDNESDAY

THURSDAY
DEAR DIARY

FRIDAY
DEAR DIARY

SATURDAY
DEAR DIARY

SUNDAY

3 THINGS I AM GRATEFUL FOR

MONDAY

TUESDAY

WEDNESDAY

THURSDAY

FRIDAY

SATURDAY

SUNDAY

I AM GRATEFUL

MONDAY
DEAR DIARY

TUESDAY

WEDNESDAY
DEAR DIARY

THURSDAY

FRIDAY

SATURDAY

DEAR DIARY

SUNDAY

DEAR DIARY

3 THINGS I AM GRATEFUL FOR

MONDAY

TUESDAY

WEDNESDAY

THURSDAY

FRIDAY

SATURDAY

SUNDAY

I AM GRATEFUL

MONDAY

TUESDAY

WEDNESDAY
DEAR DIARY

THURSDAY
DEAR DIARY

FRIDAY
DEAR DIARY

SATURDAY
DEAR DIARY

SUNDAY

3 THINGS I AM GRATEFUL FOR

MONDAY

TUESDAY

WEDNESDAY

THURSDAY

FRIDAY

SATURDAY

SUNDAY

I AM GRATEFUL

MONDAY

TUESDAY
DEAR DIARY

WEDNESDAY
DEAR DIARY

THURSDAY

FRIDAY

SATURDAY

SUNDAY

3 THINGS I AM GRATEFUL FOR

MONDAY

TUESDAY

WEDNESDAY

THURSDAY

FRIDAY

SATURDAY

SUNDAY

I AM GRATEFUL

MONDAY

TUESDAY

WEDNESDAY

THURSDAY

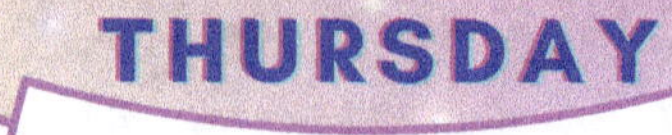

FRIDAY

SATURDAY
DEAR DIARY

SUNDAY

3 THINGS I AM GRATEFUL FOR

MONDAY

TUESDAY

WEDNESDAY

THURSDAY

FRIDAY

SATURDAY

SUNDAY

I AM
GRATEFUL

THE MORE
GRATEFUL I AM

the more beauty I see

CALENDAR

MONTH

YEAR

S	M	T	W	T	F	S

REMEMBER TO:

CALENDAR

MONTH

YEAR

S	M	T	W	T	F	S

REMEMBER TO:

CALENDAR

MONTH

YEAR

S	M	T	W	T	F	S

REMEMBER TO:

CALENDAR

MONTH

YEAR

S	M	T	W	T	F	S

REMEMBER TO:

CALENDAR

MONTH	YEAR

S	M	T	W	T	F	S

REMEMBER TO:

CALENDAR

MONTH	YEAR

S	M	T	W	T	F	S

REMEMBER TO:

CALENDAR

<table>
<tr><td>**MONTH**</td><td>**YEAR**</td></tr>
</table>

S	M	T	W	T	F	S

REMEMBER TO:

CALENDAR

MONTH	YEAR

S	M	T	W	T	F	S

REMEMBER TO:

CALENDAR

<table>
<tr><td>MONTH</td><td>YEAR</td></tr>
</table>

S	M	T	W	T	F	S

REMEMBER TO:

CALENDAR

<table>
<tr><td>MONTH</td><td>YEAR</td></tr>
</table>

S	M	T	W	T	F	S

REMEMBER TO:

CALENDAR

MONTH

YEAR

S	M	T	W	T	F	S

REMEMBER TO:

CALENDAR

MONTH

YEAR

S	M	T	W	T	F	S

REMEMBER TO:

MY VISION

GOALS & DREAMS

WEEKLY

MONTHLY

YEARLY

HOW I PLAN TO REACH MY GOALS

MY FAVORITE THINGS

MY FAVORITE SONGS

MY FAVORITE HOBBIES

MY FAVORITE BOOKS

MY FAVORITE FOODS

MY FAVORITE MOVIES

MY FAVORITE SPORTS

MY FAVORITE THINGS

MY FAVORITE COLORS

MY FAVORITE HOLIDAYS

MY FAVORITE FLOWERS

MY FAVORITE SNACKS

MY FAVORITE DRINKS

MY FAVORITE STORES

SHOW YOURSELF-GRATITUDE

- DEEP BREATHING EXERCISES.

- REPEAT YOUR POSITIVE AFFIRMATIONS OUT LOUD.

- RELAX YOUR BODY AND MIND BY MEDITATING AND RESTING.

- DO SOME JOURNALING, WRITING OR DRAWING.

- GO FOR A RUN OR A WALK OUTSIDE.

- DANCE, JUMP, OR SKIP. MAYBE LISTEN TO MUSIC WHILE YOU DO THIS.

- SIT DOWN WITH A FRIEND OR FAMILY MEMBER AND TALK ABOUT LIFE.

- READ A GOOD BOOK.

- WATCH A FUNNY MOVIE.

- PLAY A MUSICAL INSTRUMENT.

- DO ARTS AND CRAFTS.

- EAT HEALTHY FOODS, AND DRINK LOTS OF WATER.

I SHOWED GRATITUDE TO MYSELF BY:

SHOW OTHERS GRATITUDE

- BE KIND

- SMILE

- GIVE A COMPLIMENT TO A FRIEND OR FAMILY MEMBER

- ENCOURAGE OTHERS

- BE HELPFUL

- SAY THANK YOU

- GIVE OUT A KINDNESS NOTE

- WRITE OUT A LETTER OR A CARD

- DONATE ITEMS THAT YOU NO LONGER USE

- SPEND SOME EXTRA TIME WITH LOVED ONES

- HELP MOM AND DAD OUT AROUND THE HOUSE

- THANK A TEACHER FOR THEIR HARD WORK

I SHOWED GRATITUDE TO OTHERS BY:

POSITIVE AFFIRMATIONS

I AM AMAZING

I AM BEAUTIFUL

I AM CARING

I AM A DREAMER

I AM ENOUGH

I AM GRATEFUL

I AM HAPPY

I AM INTERESTING

I AM JOYFUL

I AM KIND

I AM LOVED

I AM MOTIVATED

I AM ORIGINAL

I AM POSITIVE

I AM STRONG

I AM BRAVE

I AM SMART

I AM WORTHY

I AM TALENTED

POSITIVE AFFIRMATIONS

I AM _______________________

I AM _______________________

I AM _______________________

I AM _______________________

I AM _______________________

I AM _______________________

I AM _______________________

I AM _______________________

I AM _______________________

I AM _______________________

CUT OUT CARDS

I AM
AMAZING

I AM
BEAUTIFUL

I AM
KIND

I AM
WORTHY

I AM
STRONG

I AM
LOVED

CUT OUT CARDS

GIVE OUT A KINDNESS CARD

THANK YOU

YOU ARE LOVED

I APPRECIATE YOU

I AM GRATEFUL FOR YOU

YOU ARE SPECIAL

YOU MATTER

GIVE OUT A KINDNESS CARD

blessed

grateful

so grateful!

NAME	BIRTHDAY

CELEBRATE

NAME	BIRTHDAY

3 THINGS I AM GRATEFUL FOR

MONDAY

TUESDAY

WEDNESDAY

THURSDAY

FRIDAY

SATURDAY

SUNDAY

I AM GRATEFUL

3 THINGS I AM GRATEFUL FOR

MONDAY

TUESDAY

WEDNESDAY

THURSDAY

FRIDAY

SATURDAY

SUNDAY

I AM GRATEFUL